Train Your Brain

Mindfulness Meditation For Anxiety, Depression, ADD, and PTSD

Dr Evelyn James O.K

TRAIN YOUR BRAIN

Dr Evelyn James O.K

Copyright Information

Table Of Contents

Overview

You are more than your anxiety, depression, ADD, or trauma. "Train Your Brain: Mindfulness Meditation for Anxiety, Depression, ADD, and PTSD" helps you reclaim the power of your mind. Backed by cutting-edge research, this book exposes how mindfulness strengthens the portions of your brain that manage focus, regulate emotions, and build resilience. Discover a toolkit for not just managing, but genuinely thriving – converting challenges into opportunities for growth.

Key Points:

The Science of Mindfulness: Understand how stress, anxiety, depression, and trauma commandeer your brain and discover how mindfulness practices rewire your neural pathways for enduring well-being.

Practical Meditations: Learn beginner-friendly guided meditations, including body scans, meditative strolling, and techniques for managing difficult emotions. Move beyond fundamental techniques with advanced mindfulness practices designed to target specific challenges.

Mindfulness in Everyday Life: Apply mindfulness to nutrition, communication, work, and relationships. Develop strategies for remaining present amidst distractions and managing conflict with greater awareness.

Working with Difficult Emotions: Face wrath, sorrow, and dread with skill. Cultivate self-compassion, a potent aid for navigating emotional ups and downs.

Building a Mindful Lifestyle: Create a consistent meditation practice that works for you, and learn to integrate mindfulness into all areas of your life for ongoing transformation.

This book is for you if:

- ☐ You're weary of feeling controlled by anxiety, depression, ADD, or PTSD.
- ☐ You're eager to assume an active role in your mental well-being.
- ☐ You're anxious to comprehend the science behind how mindfulness works.
- ☐ You're seeking practical tools to build resilience and discover greater serenity.
- ☐ You're weary of temporary solutions and eager for a change at the fundamental level.
- ☐ You want to understand the 'why' behind your struggles, not just suppress the symptoms.

"Train Your Brain" offers a roadmap to a life where your struggles don't define you, and where you have the power to shape your own mental and emotional landscape.

Introduction

The Limits of Quick Fixes and the Transformative Power of Mindfulness

Your brain is an extraordinary, ever-evolving machine. Yet, the relentless pace and pressures of modern life can cast its delicate balance into disarray. Anxiety tightens its grip, depression casts a long shadow, distractions from ADD scatter your focus, or the reminders of past trauma linger, disrupting your present serenity. When these conditions take root, it's not solely about difficult emotions – real, measurable changes occur within the intricate networks of your brain.

We live in a society obsessed with immediate solutions. A pill to numb the agony, a self-help app promising rapid change, and a 10-minute breathing exercise to erase a lifetime of struggle. While these tools might offer transient relief, they often fail to address the true source of mental distress. If these quick remedies were the answer, why are rates of anxiety, depression, and trauma on the rise?

The harsh reality is that the path to genuine healing necessitates a deeper approach. It requires acknowledging the astounding complexity of your brain and how chronic stress, negative thought patterns, and unprocessed experiences can etch themselves into its very structure.

This is where the transformative power of mindfulness comes in. Mindfulness meditation, backed by a growing corpus of scientific research, is like targeted exercise for your brain. It progressively strengthens the neural networks responsible for attention, emotional regulation, and resilience. This isn't just about feeling calmer in the present (though that's often a welcome side effect); mindfulness is about rewiring your brain for lasting well-being.

Imagine this: Instead of your brain feeling like a runaway train commandeered by anxiety, depression, or the disruptive patterns of ADD, you start to cultivate a sense of inner spaciousness. You gain the ability to observe your thoughts and emotions with a trace of gentle curiosity, rather than being consumed by them. From this place of awareness, a remarkable transformation begins to take place.

Mindfulness doesn't pledge to erase all your difficulties overnight. It's not a remedy for deep-rooted challenges. However, it offers something far more profound:

☐ Understanding the Brain-Mind Connection: You'll learn how your mental experiences – your racing thoughts, spiraling worries, crushing sorrow – are directly related to your brain's functioning. This scientific knowledge empowers you, demystifying your struggles.

☐ Tools for Emotional Regulation: You'll develop techniques to navigate difficult emotions, breaking free from those old, automatic reactions that leave you feeling burdened.

☐ Mental Clarity and Focus: Mindfulness strengthens your attentional spotlight, helping you combat the distractions that blight modern life, whether you have ADD or simply struggle to stay on task.

☐ Reclaiming Control: Instead of feeling like a victim of your brain, mindfulness cultivates a fundamental sense of agency. You learn that you have more discretion over your inner experience than you ever realized.

This book won't deliver you a magic solution to banish anxiety, depression, ADD, or trauma forever. What it will provide is a roadmap, rooted in science and validated by numerous individuals, to a more empowered relationship with your mind. This journey isn't about suppressing your experiences or imposing relentless positivity. Instead, it's about developing the skills to confront your challenges with greater awareness, compassion, and ultimately, a sense of control that can pave the way for lasting transformation.

Think of it like this: Imagine yourself standing at a crossroads. The well-worn path to the left promises quick fixes and transient relief but ultimately leads back to the same struggles. The path to the right, though initially less familiar, offers the potential for profound, sustainable change. This book is your guide as you embark on this new path, equipping you with the tools and practices you need to navigate the terrain and cultivate a more resilient, balanced mind.

The journey of training your brain with mindfulness is not linear. There will be moments of frustration, setbacks, and days when the lethargy seems to return. However, with consistent practice and the support offered within these pages, you'll learn to navigate these challenges with growing self-compassion. Over time, you'll witness a profound transformation in how you relate to your thoughts, emotions, and experiences. You'll develop the inner fortitude and clarity to navigate life's inevitable challenges with greater equanimity and resilience.

Part I: Understanding the Science of Mindfulness

Chapter 1: The Wandering Mind and its Consequences

Our minds are extraordinary instruments, capable of astounding feats of creativity, problem-solving, and connection. However, that same mind can also be our own worst enemy. A mind prone to relentless anxiety, crushing sorrow, scattered attention, or the lingering remnants of trauma can make commonplace life feel like an uphill battle. This chapter delves into how the benign act of a wandering mind can contribute to the vicious cycles of anxiety, depression, ADD, and PTSD, and sets the groundwork for understanding why mindfulness offers a potent way out.

How anxiety, depression, ADD, and PTSD hijack focus and well-being

Let's examine how each of these conditions can disrupt our mental landscape:

Anxiety: The Worried Mind. Anxiety is characterized by excessive concern about the future, often accompanied by physical symptoms like restlessness, tension, and difficulty sleeping. The anxious mind gets caught in a cycle of "what ifs", scanning for potential threats, and ruminating over past events. This persistent state of hypervigilance exhausts mental resources and makes it difficult to focus on the present moment.

Depression: The Downward Spiral. Depression manifests as persistent melancholy, loss of interest in activities, fatigue, and changes in sleep and appetite. The depressed mind becomes ensnared in negative thought patterns, replaying past failures and seeing the future through a dismal lens. This impairs concentration, decision-making, and overall well-being.

ADD: The Scattered Mind. Attention Deficit Disorder (ADD) makes it difficult to sustain focus, control impulses, and manage duties. The ADD mind flits from one thought to another, is readily distracted by stimuli, and struggles to remain on track. This leads to frustration, disorganization, and a sense of underachievement.

PTSD: The Haunted Mind. Post Traumatic Stress Disorder (PTSD) develops after experiencing or witnessing a profoundly distressing event. The traumatized mind becomes bound in a state of elevated alert. Flashbacks, visions, and intrusive thoughts disrupt daily life.

Hyperarousal and difficulty concentrating leave individuals feeling perpetually on edge and unable to find serenity.

The Common Thread: The Wandering Mind

Beneath these unique challenges lies a common thread: a mind that wanders away from the present moment. While it's normal for our thoughts to drift occasionally, those with anxiety, depression, ADD, and PTSD get trapped in spirals of thought with a markedly negative flavor. These beliefs are often distorted, and unhelpful, and contribute to a sense of being out of control.

Stress and the Fight-or-Flight Response

To comprehend why our minds function this way, it's useful to look back at our evolutionary past. Our minds devised a sophisticated stress response system - the "fight-or-flight" response - to help us survive threats in a perilous world. When faced with peril, this system initiates a cascade of physiological changes:

- Hormone release: Adrenaline and cortisol saturate the body, increasing heart rate, blood pressure, and breathing for rapid action.

- [ ] Resource diversion: Energy is diverted from non-essential functions like digestion towards musculature for escape or defense.
- [ ] Hypervigilance: The senses become heightened, scanning for peril and making it difficult to concentrate on anything else.

In prehistoric periods, these responses were vital. However, in modern life, most stresses are less about physical survival and more about social constraints, deadlines, or our anxieties and concerns. Our minds haven't quite caught up, often reacting as if we're confronting a saber-toothed tiger when it's just a difficult email or an unpleasant memory.

Chronic Stress: The Modern Enemy

When the fight-or-flight response is perpetually activated, even by low-level stressors, it takes a toll on both our mental and physical well-being. Chronically elevated stress hormones have been linked to a wide range of issues, including compromised immunity, cardiac problems, and mental health difficulties.

The Consequences of Chronic Stress

- [ ] Hijacked Focus: When perpetually on alert, the brain's attention centers struggle to do their job. You become easily derailed, whether it's dread escalating out of control for anxiety, or being unable to stay on task due to ADD.

☐ Emotional Dysregulation: Chronic tension wears down the brain regions responsible for managing emotions. This makes you more prone to intense anxiety, depressive lows, and the hyperarousal of PTSD.

☐ Physical Toll: Continual release of stress hormones disrupts sleep, diminishes the immune system, and increases risks for a range of health problems.

The Vicious Cycle

Mental distress itself becomes a stressor, producing a loop:

A trigger arises (difficult task, anxiety, reminder of trauma, etc.)

The fight-or-flight system steps in, flooding the body with stress hormones.

This intensifies negative thought patterns and makes focus even harder.

Perceived failure or uncontrolled thoughts add to the distress…

…Which further activates the stress response, and the cycle persists.

The Link to Mental Health

Chronic stress directly affects brain regions involved in attention, emotion regulation, and memory formation. This can make the cycles of anxiety, depression, ADD, and PTSD even more difficult to break free from.

The Path Forward

This chapter doesn't offer simple answers, but it does offer a starting point: understanding. With awareness of how our minds are constructed and how stress impacts them, we can begin to create a new relationship with our thoughts and experiences. This is where mindfulness comes in, which we'll look into in the next chapter.

Chapter 2: What is Mindfulness?

The word 'mindfulness' gets tossed around a lot these days. It's become a ubiquitous term emblazoned across magazine covers, health blogs, and wellness retreats. But beneath the fashionable veneer lurks a potent practice with origins extending back thousands of years. Mindfulness isn't just a fad; it's a fundamental principle in numerous Eastern traditions, particularly Buddhism. Originally, it wasn't intended to be a stress-reduction technique for modern professionals, but a path to increased self-awareness and enlightenment. However, the core principles of mindfulness – paying attention to the present moment with openness and inquiry – translate gorgeously into tools for navigating the complexities of 21st-century life.

Defining Mindfulness: Present-Moment Awareness

At its center, mindfulness is the simple act of paying attention to the present moment with an attitude of openness, curiosity, and non-judgment. This means noticing the totality of your experience, both internally and externally.

- Bodily Sensations: The physical sensations you experience are a bountiful source of information. Notice the weight of your body in a chair, the rise and fall of your breath in your nostrils, or any tension or relaxation in your musculature. Are you feeling energized or sluggish? Hot or cold? Mindfulness allows you to inhabit your body entirely, without taking these sensations for granted.

- Thoughts and Emotions: Our minds are continuously generating a stream of thoughts, concerns, and self-talk. In mindfulness, we observe these mental events without getting carried away by them. Imagine your thoughts like leaves floating down a stream – you can observe them pass by without attaching to any particular one. Similarly, emotions arise, fluctuate, and dwindle. Mindfulness allows us to acknowledge our emotions without judgment, creating space to respond rather than react impulsively.

- Sensory Awareness: Our senses are continuously bombarded with information – sights, sounds, scents, tastes, and textures. Mindfulness invites us to calm down and genuinely experience the world around us. Take a moment to appreciate the minutiae in your environment. What colors and shapes do you see? What sounds do you hear, pleasurable or unpleasant? Can you perceive the subtle nuances of your last drink of coffee? By engaging our senses with mindfulness, we can rediscover the beauty and richness of the present moment.

My awareness of mindfulness shifted dramatically when I came upon a book recommending a "raisin meditation." I doubted initially – what could I possibly learn from looking at dried fruit? Yet, with a sense of curiosity, I decided to give it a try. I settled into a comfortable chair, picked up a solitary raisin, and examined it attentively. The wrinkled exterior, once unremarkable, now contained a surprising complexity of textures and creases. I brought the raisin to my nostrils and inhaled its subtle sweetness. As I slipped it into my mouth, I paid close attention to the burst of flavor and the way it moved on my tongue. The whole experience took about three minutes, yet it felt like an eternity compared to the usual manner I mindlessly gulped down my food. This straightforward exercise made me realize how much I'd been racing through life on autopilot, missing the richness of the present moment. Mindfulness wasn't about emptying my mind or achieving some state of serenity; it was about slowing down, paying attention, and genuinely relishing the intricacies of my experience. From that day on, I began incorporating mindfulness practices into my daily regimen. Sometimes it would be a few meditative breaths during a stressful commute, other times it would be relishing the flavor and texture of my lunch. Gradually, I found myself becoming more present, less reactive, and able to appreciate the basic joys of ordinary life.

The Difference Between Mindfulness and Meditation

Mindfulness is the primary skill we cultivate, and meditation is the training ground where we develop that skill. Think of it like this: mindfulness is like a muscle – it's present throughout your day, but it needs exercise to become strong. Meditation is like going to the gym to train that muscle specifically. There are many distinct styles of meditation practice, each with a unique focus:

- Focused Attention Meditation: This is where you deliberately train your attention to remain on a single anchor point, such as the breath or a mantra (a repeated word or phrase). As your mind inevitably wanders (because that's what minds do!), you gingerly redirect your attention back to the anchor point. This practice strengthens your concentration and trains you to be less distracted.

- Open Awareness Meditation: Here, you cultivate a broader, more spacious awareness. Instead of focussing on a single point, you observe all your internal and external experiences – thoughts, feelings, sensations, sounds, sights, scents – with a sense of curiosity and equanimity. It's like resting on a hilltop, soaking in the entire landscape of your experience. This practice cultivates a sense of calmness and allows you to see your thoughts and emotions arise and fade away without getting wrapped up in them.

- Loving-Kindness and Compassion Meditation: These meditations cultivate positive emotions like kindness, benevolence, and compassion towards oneself and others. By actively sending out these intentions, you can begin to transform negative self-talk and develop a more compassionate and accepting relationship with yourself and the world around you.

Myths and Misconceptions About Mindfulness

Let's clarify some prevalent misunderstandings:

- Myth 1: Mindfulness is about cleansing your consciousness. Your mind will always think—that's its duty! Mindfulness is about noticing those thoughts without getting immersed in them.
- Myth 2: Mindfulness is religious. While rooted in Buddhist traditions, mindfulness is a secular practice adaptable to any

background. It's about paying attention, not subscribing to a specific belief system.

- ☐ Myth 3: Mindfulness necessitates remaining still for hours. While focused meditation sessions are beneficial, mindfulness also means bringing mindful awareness to ordinary tasks like walking, dining, or even washing dishes.
- ☐ Myth 4: Mindfulness is always being positive. Life involves complex emotions—mindfulness helps us acknowledge them without allowing them to control us.
- ☐ Scientific References

Numerous studies support the benefits of mindfulness:

Brain Changes: Research indicates mindfulness increases the density of gray matter in brain areas associated with attention, learning, and emotional regulation. ([Example study: Hölzel, B. K., et al. (2011). Mindfulness practice leads to increases in regional brain gray matter density. Psychiatry Research: Neuroimaging, 191(1), 36–43.])

Stress Reduction: Mindfulness diminishes cortisol (stress hormone) levels and helps modulate the nervous system. ([Example study: Chiesa, A., & Serretti, A. (2009). Mindfulness-based stress reduction for stress management in healthy people: A review and meta-analysis. The Journal of Alternative and Complementary Medicine, 15(5), 593–600.])

Mental Health: Mindfulness demonstrates promise in combating anxiety, and depression, and enhancing focus in those with ADD. ([Examples: Hofmann, S. G., Sawyer, A. T., Witt, A. A., & Oh, D. (2010). The effect of mindfulness-based therapy on anxiety and depression: A meta-analytic review. Journal of Consulting and Clinical Psychology, 78(2), 169–183.])

Mindfulness is a voyage, not a destination. In the next chapter, we'll look at how it alters the way your brain functions.

Chapter 3: Mindfulness and the Brain

The previous chapters examined the toll that a meandering mind can take on our well-being, and how conditions like anxiety, depression, ADD, and PTSD can manifest as a result. Now, we delve into the domain of neuroplasticity, the brain's remarkable ability to adapt and change throughout our lives. This groundbreaking discovery challenges the long-held belief that the mature brain is fixed and immutable. Instead, it reveals a dynamic organ that can be shaped by our experiences, beliefs, and practices. Mindfulness meditation emerges as an effective tool in this context. By repeatedly training your attention to focus on the present moment, you actively engage specific neural networks in your brain. Over time, these networks become strengthened, leading to a cascade of positive changes that enhance your mental well-being and emotional regulation.

Neuroplasticity and how mindfulness changes your brain

Your Brain Isn't Fixed: For a long time, scientists believed the adult brain was essentially unchangeable. However, innovative research revealed the phenomenon of neuroplasticity - your brain's remarkable ability to reorganize itself, forming new connections and even growing new neurons in response to experience.

Mindfulness as Mental Exercise: Consider mindfulness an exercise for your intellect. When you repeatedly practice focusing on the present moment, you strengthen neural networks responsible for attention, emotional regulation, and self-awareness. And like exercise, consistency is key for enduring results.

Brain regions involved in attention, emotion regulation, and self-awareness

Let's look at some essential players in your brain and how mindfulness influences them:

The Prefrontal Cortex (PFC): Often referred to as the "CEO" of your brain, the PFC is responsible for a broad range of executive functions, including focus, decision-making, impulse control, and planning. When you're bombarded with concerns or ensnared in a cycle of negative thoughts, the PFC struggles to function optimally. Mindfulness strengthens the PFC, helping you break free from rumination, reduce reactivity to emotional stimuli, and make mindful choices that align with your long-term objectives.

The Amygdala: This almond-shaped structure deep within the brain functions as your brain's alarm system, essential to the fight-or-flight response. When the amygdala perceives a threat, it initiates a cascade of physiological changes, bombarding your body with stress hormones like cortisol and adrenaline. Overactivity in the amygdala is linked to anxiety and emotional outbursts. Mindfulness helps control the amygdala, leading to greater calm amidst strong emotions. By training your attention to concentrate on the present moment, rather than pondering on past anxieties or future concerns, you can activate the calming centers of the brain and deactivate the amygdala's fight-or-flight response.

The Insula: This region hidden deep within the cerebral cortex plays a central role in interoception – the ability to sense your body's internal sensations. It incorporates information throughout your body, including pulse rate, breathing, and muscle tension. When you're agitated, for example, the insula might register a rapid pulse rate or tightness in your thorax. Mindfulness sharpens your insula, allowing you to better understand and regulate physical signs of tension or emotional distress. By becoming more aware of your body's subtle cues, you can learn to take proactive measures to regulate your stress response, such as deep breathing or progressive muscle relaxation.

The Default Mode Network (DMN): This network of brain regions becomes active when your mind wanders, often replaying past experiences or getting caught up in future concerns. It's associated with self-referential thinking, and when overactive, can contribute to rumination and feelings of isolation. Mindfulness helps silence the DMN, leading to less mental chatter and more presence in the present. By gradually drawing your attention back to the present moment when your mind wanders, you can cultivate a sense of calm and groundedness.

Research on mindfulness for reducing symptoms

The science backs it up: mindfulness isn't just about feeling happy, it produces measurable changes in the brain associated with reduced symptoms of several mental health conditions.

- Anxiety: Studies show that mindfulness-based interventions can reduce the size and reactivity of the amygdala, increase PFC activity, and help individuals manage anxiety and distress.
- Depression: Mindfulness can positively alter brain regions involved in mood regulation, decrease rumination, and increase a sense of self-compassion.

- ADD: Mindfulness enhances attention by strengthening focus networks, helping manage distractibility, and enhancing impulse control.
- PTSD: Mindfulness can help individuals with PTSD regulate overwhelming emotions, decrease flashbacks, and manage trauma triggers with greater awareness.

Important Notes:

- Mindfulness is a talent: Like any talent, it takes practice. Don't get discouraged if you don't sense immediate change – the brain adapts over time.
- Not a Cure-All: Mindfulness works best alongside other interventions like therapy and (if required) medication.

Understanding the effects of mindfulness on your brain provides potent motivation. It demonstrates that the effort you make towards your practice has a tangible impact on your mental well-being. Knowing that your brain can adapt and develop offers optimism and a sense of control amidst the challenges of mental health struggles.

Part II: The Practice of Mindfulness

Chapter 4: Getting Started

While mindfulness meditation can be practiced anytime, anywhere, creating a tranquil environment and establishing a comfortable posture will make your initial sessions more accessible and rewarding. This chapter will guide you through preparing your meditation space, finding a suitable posture, and mastering the fundamental technique of mindful breathing. Consider your meditation space a sanctuary, a dedicated place where you can cultivate inner serenity and silence amidst the daily hustle. It doesn't have to be a large, designated room – even a calm corner of your home or office will do! The key is to minimize distractions and create an ambiance that fosters relaxation and focus.

Preparing Your Space for Meditation

Ideally, locate a quiet corner of your home or business where you are less likely to be disturbed. Doesn't have to be a sizable space;

any little niche will do! Here are a few suggestions to optimize your environment:

- ☐ Minimize Distractions: Turn off your phone's notifications, close superfluous windows on your computer, and let others in your household know you'd like some undisturbed time.
- ☐ Lighting: Dim or natural lighting is usually preferable to harsh, fluorescent lights. If feasible, natural light from a window can be very soothing.
- ☐ Comfort: Choose a space where the temperature is agreeable. Have a blanket or light sweater accessible in case you get chilly during your sit.
- ☐ Optional Elements: Some individuals appreciate adding elements to create a sense of ritual. A candle, a piece of meaningful artwork, or gentle music can enhance the ambiance but aren't essential.

Finding a Comfortable Posture

Contrary to prevalent images, you don't need to contort yourself into a pretzel-like position to meditate. The key is to find a posture that is alert and relaxed. Here are a few common options, each with its benefits:

- [ ] Seated in a Chair: This is a wonderful option for novices or those with physical limitations. Find a robust chair with a straight back and a seat that allows your feet to rest level on the floor, shoulder-width apart. Avoid chairs with arms that might restrict your posture. Sit up erect with a gentle lengthening of your vertebrae, but avoid rigidity. Rest your hands gently in your lap or on your thighs, palms facing up or down, whichever feels more comfortable.

- [ ] Seated on a Cushion: A meditation cushion or folded blanket can provide support for your knees and hips, elevating your sacrum slightly above your knees. This can help maintain a natural curve in your lower spine. Sit cross-legged, positioning your right foot on top of your left thigh and your left foot on top of your right thigh (half-lotus) if this feels comfortable for your pelvis and knees. If not, you can merely sit with both legs extended in front of you (full lotus). Experiment to discover what works best for you. Again, your spine should be upright and relaxed, with your shoulders curled back and down.

- [ ] Seated on a Meditation Bench: A meditation bench provides a slightly inclined perch that can help maintain correct spinal alignment. This can be a good option for those who find it challenging to recline comfortably on the floor. As with other postures, ensure your feet are rested comfortably on the floor or a footrest.

☐ Kneeling: If reclining on the floor is uncomfortable for your knees or ankles, you can attempt kneeling. A meditation bench with a kneeling pad can be useful here. Sit back on your heels or use a zabuton (a meditation cushion) for additional support.

Ultimately, the ideal posture is the one that enables you to be both comfortable and alert during your meditation practice. Experiment with various options and discover what works best for your body.

Important Notes on Posture:

☐ distress: Some initial distress, particularly in your legs or back, is normal. Experiment with minor adjustments, but don't feel compelled to maintain picture-perfect form.

☐ Injuries or Limitations: If you have physical limitations, alter these postures accordingly. Mindfulness can still be practiced effectively while prioritizing your comfort and safety.

The Basics of Mindful Breathing

Your respiration is the foundation of mindfulness meditation. It's your ever-present anchor, always available to draw your attention back to the present moment. Here's how to begin:

- ☐ Settle into your posture: Follow the previous guidelines to find a comfortable, supported position. Allow your eyes to close gently or maintain a gentle gaze downwards a few feet in front of you.

- ☐ Notice the breath: Without attempting to change it, merely observe the natural flow of your breath. Observe the rise and fall of your abdomen, the movement of your chest, or the subtle sensations of air entering and exiting your nostrils.

- ☐ Wandering Mind: It's entirely normal for your mind to wander - that's what minds do! When you notice you've gotten distracted by a thought, emotion, or external sound, delicately acknowledge it without becoming entangled.

- ☐ Return to the Breath: Kindly redirect your attention back to the sensations of your respiration. Do this as many times as needed, without judgment. The basic act of noticing the distraction and returning is the true practice.

Helpful Tips:

- ☐ Counting Breaths: If your mind is particularly active, it can be beneficial to silently count each inhale and exhale up to ten, and then start again from one.

- ☐ Labeling: Briefly designate your thoughts as "thinking" and reorient to the breath.

Remember, this is a discipline. There's no "good" or "bad" meditation. Simply turn up, and with consistency, you'll cultivate greater awareness and comfort.

Chapter 5: Mindfulness Meditations for Beginners

In the previous chapter, we laid the foundation for your mindfulness practice – setting up your space, investigating various postures, and focusing on your breath as an anchor. Now, you're ready to investigate a variety of mindfulness meditations that can be seamlessly incorporated into your daily routine.

Body Scan Meditation

The body scan is a potent method to cultivate awareness of physical sensations in the present moment. This practice can help manage chronic pain by allowing you to observe pain sensations without judgment or resistance. By bringing your attention to the body in a non-reactive manner, you can learn to disengage from the story your mind creates around the pain. This can lead to a decreased perceived intensity of pain and a greater sense of control over your response to it.

The body scan can also promote relaxation by assisting you in identifying areas where you carry tension. As you become more aware of physical tension, you can consciously choose to release it, leading to a deeper state of physical and mental comfort.

Finally, the body scan can deepen your recognition of how tension and emotions manifest in the body. For example, you might detect tightness in your chest when you feel apprehensive, or a churning in your stomach when you're furious. By becoming more aware of these connections, you can learn to use your body as a signal system, prompting you to address emotional issues before they escalate.

Instructions:

- [ ] Settling In: Find a comfortable position reclining down or seated. It's beneficial to close your eyes, but you can keep them softly open if that feels preferable.

- [ ] Scanning the Body: Begin by bringing your attention to the heels of your left foot. Simply observe any sensations that are present – tingling, warmth, pressure, constriction, or even a sense of absence. Spend a few moments with each part of the body as you progressively bring awareness from your toes up the leg, across your pelvis, into your abdomen, chest, shoulders, arms, hands, neck, and head.

- [ ] Non-judgmental Awareness: Observe without attempting to modify or fix anything. If thoughts arise about how you're feeling, acknowledge them with phrases like "thinking", or "noticing tension" and gradually return to the sensations in your body.

- ☐ Whole Body Awareness: Once you've completed the scan, expand your awareness to include your entire body as a whole, observing the interconnectedness of your physical form.
- ☐ Variations: Experiment with scanning downward from your head to your ankles, or concentrating on areas where you hold tension.

Tips:

- ☐ Maintain a non-judgmental curiosity.
- ☐ It might feel enticing to "fix" sensations, but simply observe and release any impulse to control.

Mindful Walking Meditation

Mindful strolling transforms a simple activity into an opportunity for embodied awareness. When you feel restless or your mind requires a change of scenery, step outside and locate a quiet path. Perhaps it's a designated walking trail in a park, a tranquil hallway in your office, or even just a few paces back and forth in your living room. The key is to choose a location that allows you to wander for a few minutes without interruption.

Once you've found your location, take a moment to pause and connect with your body. Notice the sensations of your feet on the ground, the way your weight is distributed, and the natural rhythm of your respiration. As you begin to walk, apply your undivided attention to the experience. Feel the ground beneath your feet with each step – the firmness, texture, and any subtle changes as the terrain varies. Notice the way your legs move, the motion of your arms, and the subtle alterations in your balance. Engage all of your senses – listen to the sounds of your footfall, feel the breeze on your skin, and take in the images around you without getting lost in thought.

Instructions:

- ☐ Choosing Your Location: You can practice mindful strolling indoors or outdoors. Find a relatively calm path where you can walk for a few minutes without interruption.
- ☐ Begin with Posture: Before you take your first stride, halt for a moment to ground yourself. Notice your feet on the ground, your body's posture, and the sensations of your respiration.

☐ The Act of Walking: Begin by raising one foot slowly, observing the sensations of the muscles and joints in your leg. Place the foot down heel to toe, registering the contact with the earth. Shift your weight and repeat with the other foot.

☐ Expanded Awareness: As you walk, broaden your awareness to include the sensations in your whole body – the movement of your arms, and the swaying of your torso. Notice sights, scents, and sounds without getting carried away by your thoughts about them.

☐ Returning to the Present: If your mind wanders, merely guide your attention back to the sensations of walking.

Tips:

☐ Walk slowly, even slower than feels natural, to enable you time to focus on the details.

☐ No need to gaze at your feet. Keep an unhurried gaze forward.

Loving-Kindness Meditation

Loving-Kindness meditation, also known as Metta meditation, cultivates sentiments of benevolence, compassion, and acceptance toward oneself and others. It can be especially beneficial when confronting a range of negative emotions, including self-criticism, anxiety, or disconnection. By sending out these positive intentions, we not only benefit the recipient but also cultivate these positive qualities within ourselves. Research suggests that Loving-Kindness meditation can increase sentiments of happiness, reduce tension and depression, and foster stronger relationships.

Instructions:

☐ Settle in: Find a comfortable seated posture and close your eyes or soften your gaze.

☐ Phrases of Kindness: Begin by mentally reiterating phrases of kindness directed towards yourself. Some traditional phrases include:

May I be secure?

May I be happy?

May I be robust?

May I live with comfort.

☐ Extending Outwards: As you experience a sense of tenderness and compassion towards yourself, progressively expand that feeling towards others. Start with someone you love or feel gratitude for. Mentally repeat similar phrases, envisioning them as safe, healthy, and at ease. Continue expanding your circle of compassion to include neutral individuals, those you find challenging, and eventually all beings.

- ☐ Meeting Challenges: If judgments or difficult emotions arise, simply acknowledge them with compassion and return to the phrases of loving-kindness.

Tips

You might experience a genuine sense of affection, or the phrases may feel mechanical at first. Simply remain with the practice and let those sensations manifest organically.

Techniques for Working with Difficult Emotions

Mindfulness provides invaluable tools for responding skillfully to challenging emotions like fury, sorrow, fear, or anxiety. Here's a foundational practice:

- ☐ Recognize: When you observe a difficult emotion arising, name it to yourself. "There's anger," or "This is fear."

- [ ] Allow: Shift focus to the somatic sensations in your body. Where do you experience it? Is it constriction, fever, or restlessness? Observe curiously without attempting to modify it.
- [ ] Investigate: Maintain a stance of compassionate inquiry. "What thoughts accompany this feeling?" "What is the underlying message?"
- [ ] Respond, Don't React: Mindfulness empowers you to choose your response rather than reflexively reacting. Take a few mindful breaths, speak with a trusted individual, or engage in a tranquil activity.

Key Points:

- [ ] Consistency: Regular brief sessions are more beneficial than occasional lengthy ones.
- [ ] Experimentation: Be open to attempting all the techniques and discovering which suits you best.
- [ ] Compassion: The most essential element is approaching yourself with compassion.

Guided meditations for specific emotions.

Guided Meditation for Anger

Objective: To recognize anger's physical manifestations in your body, acknowledge the emotions it might be masking (like pain, frustration, or fear), comprehend its underlying message, and then release it healthily.

- ☐ Settling In: Find a comfortable but vigilant posture. Take several deep breaths, allowing tension to dissolve away on each exhale.

- ☐ Locating Anger: Scan your physique. Where do you experience anger most intensely? Is it heat in your face, tension in your chest, or a clenching in your fists? Notice without judgment.

- ☐ Observing the Sensations: Without altering anything, simply investigate these sensations. What is their quality – acute or bland, throbbing or radiating? Hold this unusual stance without attempting to control or correct anything.

- ☐ Releasing (optional): If it feels appropriate, locate a secure, private place to physically release some of the anger's energy. This could be through vigorous exercise, shredding up paper, or striking a pillow.

- ☐ Investigating the Message: Ask yourself, "If this anger could speak, what would it say?" "What needs are unmet?" Listen with compassion – fury often signals a boundary violation or injustice.

- Compassion: Extend compassion to yourself. Remember, indignation is a normal human emotion. There's no need to condemn yourself for experiencing it.
- Choosing Wise Action: Can you address the unmet need healthily? Can you set a boundary, communicate assertively, or advocate for change in the situation that provoked your anger?

Guided Meditation for Sadness

Objective: To acknowledge and venerate sorrow without getting swept away by it. This means creating space for the emotion to exist, allowing the tears to flow freely if they arise, and recognizing that melancholy is a natural human response to loss, disappointment, or grief. It's also essential to cultivate self-compassion during this time. Imagine cradling a younger version of yourself who is feeling melancholy. What words of solace and comprehension would you offer that child? Now, with the same tenderness, offer those same words to yourself. You are worthy of affection and support, even amid sorrow.

- Settling In: Choose a restful position, perhaps reclining down with a blanket. If emotions arise, let them flow freely.

☐ Where is Sadness?: Where do you feel sorrow most intensely in your body? Is it a heaviness in your chest, a constriction in your larynx, or hollowness in your stomach?

☐ Spaciousness: Allow your awareness to expand around these sensations, creating space for them. Imagine a boundless blue sky that can sustain even the most potent storm clouds.

☐ Nurture: Picture a younger version of yourself or a beloved companion that needs solace. What words of compassion would you offer? Now, tenderly propose those same words to yourself.

☐ Boundaries with Sadness: Acknowledge, "This sorrow is present right now, and it's acceptable. It will not last eternally."

☐ Returning: Gently return your awareness to your respiration and the sensations of your body in the present moment. Before opening your eyes, take a few minutes to appreciate any alterations in your state.

Guided Meditation for Fear

Objective: To calm the nervous system, differentiate between realistic and unrealistic concerns, and cultivate resilience.

☐ Settling In: Find a supportive posture, perhaps with your back against a wall or a bolster for a sense of grounding.

- The Body's Signals: Where do you sense anxiety in your body? Is it a racing pulse, tightness in the stomach, or shallow breathing? Observe with curiosity.

- Soothing the Nervous System: Place a palm on your abdomen. Focus on slow, deep inhalation, extending your exhalation. Imagine each out-breath calming your system like waves receding.

- Is the Fear Realistic?: Ask yourself, "Is there a real, present-moment threat, or is my mind anticipating something that might happen?" If it's the latter, remind yourself, "This is my mind creating a possible future."

- Building Resilience: Recall a time you faced a challenge and surmounted it. Bring to mind the fortitude you discovered in that time. Tell yourself, "I can manage what comes. I am inventive."

- Grounding: Focus on the sensations of your body making contact with the ground or chair. This reminds you of your present-moment safety.

Guided Meditation for Anxiety

Objective: To transition from apprehensive thoughts to the present-moment experience of the body and senses.

- [ ] Settling In: Find a comfortable posture and soften your focus.

- [ ] Mindful Movement: Choose a basic, repetitive movement – walking, undulating, or rubbing your thumb and forefinger together. Notice the minute sensations produced by the movement.

- [ ] The 5 Senses: Engage your senses one by one. Consider the following: five things you can see, four things you can hear, three things you can touch, two things you can smell, and one item you can taste.

- [ ] Anchoring in the Breath: When apprehensive thoughts return, observe them without judgment and gently redirect your attention to the physical sensations of your breath moving in and out of your body.

- [ ] Spaciousness: As you settle into the present, observe the space between thoughts. Observe that you are not your thoughts, and they come and go like clouds.

Important Note: If any of these emotions feel overwhelming, seek support from a therapist.

Remember, these meditations are designed for you to explore and adapt to suit your requirements. Embrace them as a tool for self-discovery and increased well-being.

Chapter 6: Advanced Techniques

Having examined a variety of mindfulness meditations, you're now equipped to progress into more subtle, introspective practices. These advanced techniques offer potent tools for understanding the inner workings of your mind and skillfully traversing the complexities of anxiety, depression, ADD, PTSD, and other mental health challenges.

Open Awareness Meditation

Open awareness meditation, sometimes referred to as "choiceless awareness," entails a broadening of your attention to incorporate the totality of your experience in the present moment. This includes not only the sensations of your breath or body but also fleeting thoughts, emotions, and external stimuli. Just imagine your mind as a vast, open field. Thoughts, emotions, and sensations originate like fleeting clouds drifting across the sky. You observe them with a sense of detached inquiry, without judgment or attachment. You don't attempt to control or manipulate your experience in any way. The practice is merely to be present with whatever arises, moment by moment.

- ☐ Settling In: Find a comfortable posture and calm your attention. It's useful to commence with a few minutes of focus on the breath to anchor your attention before transitioning to open awareness.

- ☐ Spacious Awareness: Allow your awareness to expand – as if your mind is becoming a boundless, expansive sky. Instead of latching onto any particular experience, merely observe the ever-changing flux of your inner world.

- ☐ Non-attachment: Thoughts, emotions, and sensations will naturally arise. Notice them, acknowledge them like passing clouds, and allow them to dissipate without grasping onto them or getting trapped in narratives.

- ☐ Returning to Spaciousness: If your attention narrows down to a specific thought or emotion, gently relinquish your focus and return to the sense of spacious, open awareness.

Benefits of Open Awareness:

- ☐ Develops greater equanimity and non-reactivity to experiences.

- ☐ Enhances your ability to observe the workings of your mind with greater objectivity.

- ☐ Cultivates a sense of interior calm even amidst tumultuous thoughts or emotions.

Our thought patterns play a significant role in how we experience anxiety, depression, ADD, and other mental health challenges. Mindfulness of thoughts allows you to analyze the nature of your thinking with greater clarity and discern helpfulness from detrimental thought patterns. For instance, when confronting apprehension, you might find yourself engaging in catastrophizing thoughts, blowing a minor inconvenience out of proportion, and envisioning the worst-case scenario. Or perhaps depression leads you to ruminate on past failures, fueling feelings of inadequacy and worthlessness. With mindfulness of thoughts, you can observe these patterns without judgment and challenge their validity. Are these ideas realistic? Are they based on evidence, or are they distorted by fear or negativity bias? By analyzing your thinking with detached awareness, you can begin to loosen the hold of unhelpful thought patterns and cultivate more balanced, resourceful perspectives.

- ☐ Observing Thoughts: Begin by settling into either focused respiration awareness or open awareness.
- ☐ Labeling: When thoughts arise, silently designate them as "thinking". This establishes a small distance between you and the content of the thought, allowing you to disengage from becoming caught up in the storyline.

- Investigating Patterns: Observe recurrent thought patterns. Do they tend to be negative, self-critical, or catastrophizing? Notice how these patterns impact your emotional state.
- Letting Go: See if you can release your grasp on thoughts, regarding them like fleeting images on a screen rather than truths about yourself or your situation.

Benefits of Mindfulness of Thoughts

- Diminishes the power of negative reasoning, creating space for more balanced perspectives.
- Reduces rumination and anxiety.
- Enhances self-awareness and comprehension of your mental patterns.

Using Mindfulness to Understand Triggers for Anxiety, etc.

Mindfulness becomes a potent tool for recognizing the situational and internal triggers that heighten anxiety, depression, ADD flare-ups, or trauma reactivation. With enhanced awareness, you can implement preemptive strategies for managing these challenges. Here's how to practice:

- ☐ Recall a Recent Trigger: Think of a specific situation or experience that recently prompted a strong emotional reaction. It could be a disagreement, an overwhelming task, or a reminder of a traumatic event.

- ☐ Internal Scanning: Replay the situation in your mind. With a compassionate, investigative posture, observe how your thoughts, physical sensations, and emotions changed in the lead-up to the trigger. Did you observe any early warning signs that you tend to overlook?

- ☐ Pattern Recognition: Observe your pattern of reactivity. Do you tend to suppress your emotions until they explode? Get trapped in repetitive concern spirals? Freeze up or evade the situation altogether?

- ☐ Mapping Your Triggers: It can be useful to maintain a journal to track your triggers and responses. This enables you to identify common patterns and devise more effective coping strategies.

Empowerment Through Understanding

By mindfully observing your triggers, you obtain crucial insights. This self-knowledge offers vital information. You can:

- ☐ Avoid or Plan: Modify your environment to reduce exposure to triggers when possible, or prepare in advance for encounters with unavoidable triggers.
- ☐ Develop Coping Mechanisms: Identify mindfulness practices, grounding techniques, or soothing activities that effectively alleviate emotional surges.
- ☐ Challenge Your Thinking: Examine your internal dialogues around triggers. Can you substitute automatic thought patterns with more realistic or useful perspectives?

Important Note: Working with deep-seated trauma triggers often necessitates the guidance of a qualified mental health professional. Mindfulness can be a valuable complementary practice within the context of therapy.

Advanced techniques with a specific emphasis on anxiety, melancholy, ADD, and PTSD.

Anxiety

Mindfulness of Anxiety Sensations: Instead of focusing solely on anxious thoughts, pay close attention to the physical manifestations of anxiety. Often, anxiety shows up as tightening in the chest, rapid pulse, shallow respiration, or restlessness. By mindfully observing these sensations without attempting to alter them, they often lessen in intensity. You can further combine this with tranquil breathwork, such as diaphragmatic breathing, to modulate your nervous system.

Exposure-Based Mindfulness: If you have specific phobias or social anxiety, progressively introducing yourself to the feared stimulus in a secure, controlled environment while practicing mindfulness can be extremely powerful. This enables you to confront your fears while developing the ability to remain present with the discomfort without judgment. Always consult with a therapist before undertaking exposure-based approaches.

Depression

Mindfulness of Rumination: Depression often entails repetitive negative thought cycles. Mindfulness of impulses, as outlined in the previous chapter, is crucial. Additionally, investigate the emotional tone that accompanies these notions. Is it a sensation of heaviness, desolation, or hopelessness? Acknowledge this feeling and investigate any associated body sensations, offering yourself compassion amidst the experience.

Behavioral Activation with Mindfulness: Depression can deplete vitality and motivation. Mindfully observe any resistance towards engaging in daily duties or activities that once pleased you. Use modest, achievable measures to surmount inertia. Mindfully engage in these activities, paying attention to any subtle shifts in mood or vitality.

ADD

Moment-to-Moment Focus: When your mind jumps from task to task, tenderly but decisively draw your attention back to the present task. Label distractions as "thinking" and redirect. Start with brief intervals of mindful focus and progressively increase them.

Mindful Transitions: Those with ADD often struggle with transitioning between duties. Before altering gears, take a few mindful breaths. Notice any mental clutter from the previous task and allow it to subside before commencing the new one.

Mindfulness in Daily Activities: Bring a mindful awareness to routine tasks like cleansing your teeth or scrubbing dishes. Focus on the basic sensations of your body in motion or the feel of water on your palms. This anchors you in the present and trains your attentional skills.

PTSD

Grounding Techniques: When recollections or overwhelming emotions arise, grounding techniques bring your focus into the present moment. Mindfully engage with your five senses by noticing your surroundings, concentrating on tactile sensations (like the feeling of fabric against your skin), or utilizing calming fragrances like lavender.

Mindful Self-Compassion: PTSD often involves feelings of shame, self-blame, or emotional numbing. Cultivating self-compassion is crucial. Gently remind yourself that you are not to fault for what happened and deserve to feel secure and at peace. Loving-kindness meditation can be especially beneficial.

Working with a Therapist: Since PTSD is multifaceted, mindfulness is most effective when integrated into professional trauma-informed therapy. Mindfulness skills can empower you to navigate intense emotions and regain a sense of agency, while also supporting the process of therapy.

Important Reminders

- ☐ Gradual Progression: Advanced techniques require practice. Start with shorter sessions and those that feel less challenging.
- ☐ Compassionate Acceptance: Challenging days are inevitable. Treat setbacks as opportunities to learn rather than failings.
- ☐ Professional Support: For trauma and other complex diagnoses, seeking guidance from a qualified mental health professional who is knowledgeable about mindfulness is crucial.

Remember, self-awareness is a potent first step towards creating enduring change in your relationship with mental health challenges.

Part III: Applying Mindfulness in Daily Life

Chapter 7: Mindful Eating

Many of us find ourselves turning to food for reasons beyond physical hunger. We seek solace in sweets when feeling anxious, find ourselves passively snacking when bored, or use food as a distraction from challenging emotions. While these behaviors might bring transient relief, they often lead to feelings of guilt, low energy, and a sense of disconnection from our bodies and true needs.

Mindful dining offers a compassionate, transformative alternative. It helps you cultivate a healthy and enjoyable relationship with food. By becoming fully present while eating, you can tune into your body's internal cues, make conscious choices, and savor the experience.

Stress Eating and Emotional Eating

Stress eating and emotional eating are two typical habits that mindfulness can help you handle. Let's explore them in more detail:

- Stress Eating: When we're under chronic stress, our bodies release the hormone cortisol. Cortisol not only increases alertness and blood sugar levels to help us cope with the perceived threat, but it also stimulates cravings for sugary, fatty, and salty foods, which might deliver a rapid boost of energy and pleasure. Unfortunately, these types of foods often lead to a blood sugar crash later on, leaving you feeling drained and more susceptible to further cravings. This creates a vicious cycle, where stress triggers unhealthy eating habits, which in turn, can exacerbate stress levels due to feelings of guilt, shame, and low energy.

- Emotional Eating: Food can become a way to numb, soothe, or avoid difficult emotions. You might reach for a sugary pick-me-up when feeling sad, use food as a reward for a stressful day, or mindlessly snack to fill a void of boredom or loneliness. The problem with emotional eating is that it fails to treat the underlying emotional issue. The feelings of sadness, stress, or boredom are still there, and often become amplified by the guilt and shame associated with overeating.

How to spot signs of stress or emotional eating:

- ☐ Eating when not physically famished
- ☐ Craving specific foods, usually elevated in sugar, sodium, or fat
- ☐ Eating swiftly without paying attention
- ☐ Feeling disconnected or inert during or after dining
- ☐ Experiencing remorse or humiliation after eating

Consequences of Mindless Eating

While turning to food for solace is comprehensible, the long-term consequences can be significant. Consider the impact on your physical health: weight fluctuations as mindless eating often lead to consuming unnecessary calories; digestive issues as rushed eating disrupts the body's natural digestive processes; and an increased risk of chronic health conditions such as obesity, type 2 diabetes, and heart disease. Mindless consumption can also negatively impact your mental and emotional well-being. The cycle of overeating followed by negative self-talk can erode self-esteem and contribute to feelings of anxiety and depression. Furthermore, mindless eating disconnects you from the wisdom of your body. You lose touch with your natural hunger and fullness cues, making it difficult to eat in a way that nourishes and sustains you. Perhaps most concerning is that mindless eating doesn't address the underlying emotional issues that trigger unhealthy eating patterns. If you're using food to cope with stress, boredom, or sadness, those feelings will still be there, and may even worsen over time as food becomes your primary coping mechanism.

Developing a Mindful Relationship with Food

Mindful eating transforms your relationship with eating from one of automatic reactivity to one of empowered, conscious choice. It's a journey of self-discovery, helping you reconnect with the wisdom of your body and cultivate a sense of peace around food. Here's how to begin:

- Pause and Reflect: When the urge to eat arises, instead of acting on autopilot, pause and check in with yourself. Ask yourself: "Am I truly experiencing physical hunger? Or is there an underlying emotion driving me towards food?" Is it tension, boredom, sorrow, or perhaps even a craving for social connection? By taking a mindful moment, you can identify the trigger and make a conscious choice about how to respond. If it's true hunger, wonderful! Prepare a nourishing meal or snack. If it's an emotion, acknowledge it with kindness and explore healthier ways to address it.

Perhaps a few deep breaths, a call to a trusted friend, or a short walk in nature can be more helpful than reaching for food.

☐ Engage Your Senses: Before diving into your food, truly savor the experience. Notice the colors, textures, and aromas. Take a few moments to appreciate the origin of the cuisine and the effort involved in its preparation.

☐ Slow Down: Eat slowly, with complete attention to each morsel. Put your utensil down between pieces, chew thoroughly, and relish the various flavors and textures.

☐ Tune into Your Body: Pay attention to the physical sensations throughout your meal. Notice the subtle growling of hunger, the progressive sensation of fullness and satisfaction. Stop when you feel comfortably full, avoiding over-stuffed discomfort.

☐ Non-Judgmental Awareness: If you find yourself consuming for emotive reasons, practice self-compassion. Acknowledge what you're experiencing, and gently explore: What emotion am I attempting to manage?

☐ Are there healthier methods to resolve this emotion?

☐ Seek Alternative Coping Strategies: Develop a toolkit of alternative coping mechanisms for managing tension, sorrow, or boredom. Deep breathing, gentle movement, journaling, or spending time in nature can provide healthful outlets for coping with difficult emotions.

Important Reminders:

- Mindful Eating Does Not Mean Deprivation: Permit yourself to appreciate your favored foods! The key is to appreciate them thoroughly, with awareness and moderation.
- This is a Practice, Not Perfection: There will be occasions when you lapse back into old habits. Be compassionate with yourself and return to mindful dining whenever you feel ready.

Benefits of Mindful Eating

Mindful eating uncovers a multitude of benefits, extending far beyond weight management:

- Enhanced Digestion: Mindful dining promotes a tranquil state, ideal for optimal digestion and nutrient absorption.
- Improved Portion Control: Increased awareness of hunger and fullness signals helps you consume the right amount for your body's requirements.
- Greater Satisfaction: Savoring food entirely leads to unexpected levels of enjoyment and less desire to overeat.

☐ Freedom from Guilt: Mindful eating cultivates a non-judgmental approach to your choices, nurturing self-compassion and serenity of mind.

☐ Empowered Choices: You recognize the power to break unhealthy eating behaviors and make conscious decisions about your food.

Mindful dining is not a diet but a lifelong practice that fosters a healthier, more harmonious relationship with nutrition.

Chapter 8: Mindful Communication

Mindfulness isn't just about silent meditation. It's a way of being that permeates every aspect of your existence, including the way you communicate with others. Mindful communication involves cultivating a quality of presence, a willingness to genuinely listen, and the ability to manage your own emotions within challenging conversations. This chapter will examine how mindfulness empowers you to engage with those around you with greater empathy, understanding, and skill.

Mindful communication starts with intentionality. Before delving into a discourse, take a few moments to center yourself. Remind yourself of the significance of genuinely listening to the other person, and setting aside your agenda for the moment. This brief halt allows you to approach the interaction with a beginner's mind, open to what the other person has to say without preconceived notions or judgments.

Truly Listening and Being Present in Conversations

All too often, our conversations resemble monologues more than dialogues. We speak without genuinely listening, waiting for our turn to communicate, or mentally formulating a rebuttal. This self-absorption creates a disconnect and hinders genuine connection. Mindfulness offers an antidote to this form of preoccupied, reactive communication. Here's how to cultivate mindful listening:

- ☐ Set an Intention: Before engaging in a discourse, take a few moments to center yourself. Remind yourself of the significance of genuinely listening to the other person, suspending your agenda for the moment. This enables you to approach the interaction with an open mind and genuine inquiry about their perspective.

- ☐ Minimize Distractions: Put aside your phone, turn off notifications, and choose a tranquil, private space for important conversations. This demonstrates respect for the speaker and allows you to completely devote your attention to their words and nonverbal cues.

- ☐ Non-Verbal Cues: Make eye contact (to a degree that feels culturally appropriate), and maintain a relaxed, open posture. These subtle indicators signal to the speaker that you are present and engaged in the conversation.

- ☐ Reflect: Practice mirroring or paraphrasing what the other person has said. This helps ensure that you're comprehending accurately and demonstrates that you're authentically interested in their message. You can use phrases like, "It sounds like you're feeling..." or "If I'm hearing you correctly, you're saying..."

☐ Curiosity over Judgment: When the speaker reveals something you disagree with, resist the impulse to immediately formulate a counterargument. Instead, approach their perspective with inquiry. Ask clarifying queries to acquire a deeper understanding of their experience. What are the thoughts, sentiments, and requirements underlying their words?

Power of Deep Listening

Deep attentiveness is remarkably potent. It strengthens relationships by fostering a sense of connection, validation, and trust. When you feel genuinely heard and understood, you're more likely to extend the same courtesy to your conversation companion. This creates a secure space for open communication, where both parties feel comfortable expressing themselves authentically. Deep listening also allows for more constructive problem-solving. When you can see a situation from another's perspective, you gain valuable insights and can devise solutions that address everyone's requirements. Imagine a couple contending with a disagreement about finances. The wife might be feeling concerned about long-term security, while the spouse prioritizes short-term enjoyment. Through thorough listening, they can uncover these underlying concerns and work together to create a budget that feels secure and allows for some enjoyment. Deep listening isn't just about passively assimilating information; it's about actively engaging with the speaker's message. By reflecting on key points, asking clarifying questions, and offering nonverbal indicators of attentiveness, you demonstrate that you're invested in understanding their world.

Managing Conflict Mindfully

Conflict is an inevitable part of life, whether navigating minor disagreements or significant tensions within relationships. Mindfulness isn't about averting conflict, but about approaching it with awareness and skill to mitigate escalation and maximize the opportunity for resolution.

- ☐ Recognizing Reactivity: Learn to identify the early warning signs of emotional reactivity. Increased heart rate, tense musculature, the urge to interrupt or lash out – observe these within yourself.
- ☐ Take a Pause: If you can, excuse yourself and take a mindful respite. Focus on your breath, exercise a brief body scan, or

even step outside to create space between the trigger and your response.

☐ Investigate Emotions: Mindfully analyze your underlying emotions. Beneath the anger, you might discover injury or anxiety. Identifying these fundamental emotions can help you respond from a less reactive place.

☐ Choose Your Words: Before speaking, ask yourself, "Is what I'm about to say helpful, true, and necessary?" If not, rephrase or delay until you've regained composure.

☐ "I" Statements: Structure your communication using "I" statements to express your sentiments and needs without blame. Instead of "You always make me feel…" try "When this happens, I feel…"

☐ Seeking to Understand: Even when experiencing strong emotions, maintain a thread of fascination about the other person's perspective. What are their underlying requirements and concerns?

Mindfulness Fosters Collaborative Problem-Solving

When both parties approach conflict mindfully, it transforms the dynamic from a power struggle into a collaborative exploration of solutions. Even if the full resolution isn't immediate, mindfulness can open the door to rebuilding connection and moving forward more constructively.

Important Considerations:

- ☐ Setting Boundaries: Mindfulness doesn't mean tolerating cruelty or disrespect. It's crucial to set firm boundaries around what treatment you will and won't tolerate.
- ☐ Knowing Your Limits: With profoundly entrenched conflict patterns, professional help may be necessary. Couples counseling or mediation can provide a secure space to address complex issues under the guidance of a skilled therapist.

Mindfulness isn't about becoming a faultless communicator overnight. It's an ongoing practice. Each time you choose to listen intently, navigate a difficult conversation with awareness, or respond to conflict with a little more skill, you're strengthening your 'mindfulness muscles' and cultivating more harmonious, fulfilling relationships.

Chapter 9: Mindfulness at Work (or School)

The workplace and classroom can be breeding grounds for worry, distraction, and mental overload. Whether it's demanding deadlines, multitasking overload, challenging peers, the pressure of tests, or social worries, our mental well-being is often put to the test. Mindfulness isn't about turning off the outside world - it's about finding better balance and attention within it. This chapter will give you practical strategies for bringing mindfulness into your daily work or school routine, allowing you to thrive amidst even the most hectic of days.

Staying Focused Amidst Distractions

The nature of modern work and study demands our attention in a million different ways. Multitasking has become a badge of honor, but the study shows it diminishes our efficiency and brain function. Constant email alerts, social media posts, and the draw of a second screening all add to a scattered mind. Mindfulness offers an invaluable tool for enhancing your attention and lowering the effect of external and internal distractions. Here's a two-pronged approach: handling outward distractions and managing internal distractions.

Managing External Distractions

- ☐ devoted workplace: If possible, build a devoted workplace that reduces sensory overload. This might mean decluttering your desk, choosing a quiet spot, or using noise-canceling headphones if you work in a busy setting.
- ☐ Technology Tactics: Minimize digital distractions by closing needless tabs, silencing your phone's alerts, and setting specific times for checking email rather than constantly being pulled into it.
- ☐ Communicating Your Needs: If possible, share your desire for focused time with friends or family members. Let them know when you need uninterrupted focus and set acceptable limits around your availability.

Managing Internal Distractions

Often, our thoughts are the biggest causes of distraction. They constantly churn out thoughts, fears, to-do lists, and judgments, pulling our attention away from the task at hand. Here's how to use awareness to handle them:

- Mindful Monitoring: The first step is to develop awareness of your mental concerns. Pay attention to what pulls your focus away – is it a nagging worry about an upcoming deadline, a critical inner voice, or simply the draw of checking social media? Once you find the recurring trends, you can begin to solve them.

- Non-judgmental Observation: When a distracting thought emerges, watch it with a curious, non-judgmental stance. Label it internally as "thinking" or "worrying" and notice its presence without getting involved in its content.

- Letting Go: Just like real things in your hand, thoughts tend to arise and then dissipate. Practice letting go of distracting thoughts without holding on to them or trying to push them away. Breath can be a powerful support here. As you become more skilled at watching and releasing distracting thoughts, you'll find it easier to keep focus on the job at hand.

- The Power of the Present Moment: Mindfulness teaches us to gently shift our attention back to the present moment. This might involve focusing on the feelings of your breath, the physical sensations in your body as you work, or the sights and sounds of your immediate surroundings. By grounding yourself in the present, you build a basis for sustained attention and productivity.

- ☐ The S.T.O.P. Practice: When you feel yourself getting pulled away by a thought or worry, try this quick practice:

Stop: Pause whatever you're doing, even just for a few moments.

Take a breath: Take a few focused breaths, focusing on the feelings of your inhale and exhale.

Observe: What's going on in your subconscious and body? Acknowledge any thoughts, feelings, or sensations.

Proceed: With renewed understanding, choose how to proceed. Can you successfully redirect your attention to the job at hand? Is a short break necessary?

- ☐ Catch and Release: When distracting thoughts appear, notice them, mentally name them as "thinking," and return to your anchor (often your breath, but it could be the feelings in your body). Practice this frequently, like light reps at the gym for your "attention muscle."

- ☐ Task Chunking: Break down big jobs into smaller, more doable chunks. This gives you a better sense of direction and lowers the overwhelm that leads to distraction.

Taking short, mindful breaks throughout your job or study sessions can greatly improve your focus, mood, and general well-being. Here are a few techniques:

Micro-Breaks

These take just a minute or two and can easily be worked into your routine:

- ☐ Mindful Minute: Set a timer for one minute. Close your eyes or soften your look and shift your full attention to your breath.
- ☐ Body Awareness: Consciously stretch, shake out any stiffness, or get up to move around quickly. Hear how your body feels.
- ☐ Senses Walk: Take a thoughtful walk around the office or outside. Pay attention to the sights, sounds, and smells around you without getting lost in thought.
- ☐ Slightly Longer Breaks (5-10 minutes)

Try these when you have a bit more time:

- [ ] Guided Meditation: Use an app like Calm or Headspace, or find a recording online to take you through a mindfulness exercise suited to your needs.
- [ ] Loving-Kindness: Especially helpful if you're facing relationship stress. Practice sending thoughts of kindness and care towards yourself or others.
- [ ] Gratitude Break: Take 5 minutes to jot down at least three things you are grateful for. This changes your viewpoint and promotes positive feelings.

Important Considerations:

- [ ] Schedule Breaks: Don't just wait until you feel overloaded. Preventative breaks are far more successful.
- [ ] Set Reminders: Utilize phone apps or calendar alerts to tell you to take short pauses.
- [ ] Get Buy-In: If possible, explain the value of mindfulness breaks to your boss or teachers. A workplace that supports well-being projects reaps benefits such as improved production and retention.

Mindfulness is a skill acquired over time. Start small, adopt what works for you, and gradually you will notice the transformative benefits in your ability to handle the stress and distractions of work or school with greater focus, clarity, and ease.

Chapter 10: Mindfulness for Difficult Emotions

Emotions like anger, sorrow, and fear are natural and inevitable aspects of the human experience. Yet, for those struggling with anxiety, depression, ADD, or PTSD, these emotions may feel especially overwhelming or even debilitating. Mindfulness provides a unique approach to coping with difficult emotions by altering your relationship with them. Instead of attempting to suppress or avoid them, you learn to approach these emotions with inquiry and compassion. In the process, you can mitigate their intensity and develop greater inner resilience.

Working with Anger, Sadness, and Fear

When powerful feelings appear, our instinct may be to fight them, engage in unhealthy coping strategies like numbing or distraction, or respond impulsively in ways we later regret. Mindfulness offers a different method – one based on self-awareness and self-regulation.

Mindfulness in Action

- ☐ Recognize and Name: When you notice a surge of anger, sadness, or fear, take a moment to recognize the emotion and its matching physical feelings in the body. Naming your feelings (e.g., "This is anger," "This is a wave of sadness," "Fear is here right now") creates a sense of detachment and breaks automatic reaction.

- ☐ Observe the feelings: Shift your attention to the physical feelings connected with the emotion, exploring with interest. Notice heat or strain, stiffness, restlessness, tightness in the chest, and a knot in the stomach. Don't judge the feelings as "good" or "bad," simply watch.

- ☐ Breathe into It: Return to conscious breathing as a support. Allow breathing to relieve areas of physical stress. Remember, feelings are like waves – they arise, peak, and finally subside.

- ☐ Investigate Triggers and Thoughts: Once the original intensity has decreased, slowly explore what sparked the feeling. Note the thoughts that accompany it. Are they reasonable, or do they represent distortions like catastrophizing?

- ☐ Compassionate Response: Choose how to react to the feeling in a way that's both skilled and connected with your values. You may need to set a limit, express yourself assertively, engage in self-care, or simply allow the feeling to run its course and pass through.

Here Are Some Specific Techniques

- ☐ rage: If rage feels overwhelming, pair focused observation with physical release. Try controlled bursts of exercise (running, jumping jacks), tearing up old scrap paper, or releasing anxiety through a stress ball.
- ☐ Sadness: Sadness often appears as heaviness in the body. Allow yourself to cry, participate in comforting activities (taking a warm bath, listening to relaxing music), or seek support from a loved one.
- ☐ Fear: If fear leads to a racing mind and physical worry, practice calming methods. Focus on your senses – the feeling of your feet on the floor, the sights around you, smells in the air. Remind yourself of what IS safely present in the current moment.

Developing Self-Compassion

Self-compassion is perhaps the most useful skill for managing difficult feelings. When we treat ourselves with the same kindness and understanding we would offer a loved one dealing with a similar situation, we soften the harsh judgments that often increase pain. Self-compassion isn't about self-pity or absolving yourself of duty. Rather, it's about understanding our shared humanity – that we all face challenges, failures, and mental pain. It's about acknowledging that suffering is part of the human experience and approaching ourselves with the same understanding and care we would give to a friend going through a tough time.

Consider this: you wouldn't berate a friend for feeling sad after a breakup or angry after being abused. You'd listen with empathy, offer words of comfort, and tell them of their natural worth. Extending this same kindness and understanding towards ourselves is the core of self-compassion.

Cultivating Self-Compassion

- Self-Kindness vs. Self-Criticism: Pay attention to your inner critic and the harsh things you tell yourself when difficult feelings arise. Counter these critical thoughts with words of self-kindness (e.g., "Everyone experiences sadness sometimes," "I'm doing my best to cope").

- ☐ Common Humanity: Remember, you're not alone. All humans face difficult feelings. Practice words like, "This is part of being human," or "Everyone experiences anger from time to time."
- ☐ Soothing Touch: Place a hand on your heart or wherever you feel comfortable. Notice the softness of your touch as it sends a safety warning to your nervous system.
- ☐ Compassionate Imagery: Imagine someone you feel deep concern for – a close friend, a beloved pet, or a spiritual figure. Extend that sense of total care and love towards yourself.

The Benefits of Self-Compassion

Research shows that self-compassion:

Reduces self-criticism and shame, which increase tough feelings.

Increases mental resilience, making it easier to manage life's obstacles.

Foster's self-acceptance, embracing both our skills and flaws.

Important Reminder: Self-compassion is a habit. Especially if you've been hard on yourself for a long time, be careful and gentle in building this skill. Every little act of kindness towards yourself matters.

Mindfulness and difficult feelings may seem like an odd pairing, but it is within these difficulties that mindfulness practice proves strong. By approaching your inner world with curiosity and kindness, you'll discover your capacity to weather life's natural storms with less stress.

Part IV: Mindfulness as a Lifestyle

Chapter 11: Building a Consistent Practice

You've found the promise of mindfulness, experienced the benefits, and perhaps even seen glimpses of the transformative power it holds. But like any skill, mindfulness needs to be developed through constant practice to truly change your way of being and connecting to the world. This chapter will address the value of regular meditation and provide practical strategies for overcoming the obvious hurdles you'll experience.

The Importance of Regular Meditation

The true magic of awareness comes through regular practice. Think of it like physical training. A single workout won't change your fitness level. You might feel a little sore the next day, but that soreness is a sign that tiny tears are being mended in your muscles, making them stronger. Consistent exercise, on the other hand, gradually improves your muscles and cardiovascular system, leading to lasting changes in your general health and fitness.

Similarly, regular mindfulness practice strengthens the neural pathways in your brain linked with focus, attention control, emotional regulation, and self-awareness. Over time, these reinforced routes can lead to lasting good changes. Consider the example of a dirt path through a field. An odd walk might leave a faint mark in the grass, but constant travel along that road over time will carve a deep, well-defined trail. Regular mindfulness practice carves brain paths that make it easier to stay focused, control feelings carefully, and react to challenges with greater awareness and calm.

- ☐ Improves Your 'Mindfulness Muscles': Just as weightlifting grows muscle, regular meditation improves your attention, emotional regulation, and self-awareness skills. This makes it easier to stay steady and non-reactive in the face of life's difficulties.

- ☐ Habit Formation: Consistent exercise helps awareness become a habit. The more you do it, the less effort it takes and the more easily you'll turn to mindfulness skills throughout the day.

- ☐ Cumulative Effects: While even short routines offer benefits, longer and more frequent sessions increase your results. Think of it like drops of water slowly eroding a stone — consistent practice can change deeply ingrained thought patterns and emotional reactions.

☐ Enhanced Self-Awareness: Regular awareness helps you to see the small changes in your thoughts, feelings, and actions over time. This self-understanding helps you become more involved in controlling your well-being.

How Often and How Long to Practice?

Ideally, aim for daily meditation. Even a few minutes can make something different. Start with what feels doable, perhaps just 2-3 minutes a day. As your practice becomes more integrated into your routine, gradually increase the length of your lessons. There's no magic number; the key is constancy. Five minutes a day is significantly more helpful than an hour-long weekly meditation if it helps you develop a regular habit of practice. Think of building your awareness muscle – small, regular workouts are more effective than sporadic, intense lessons.

Here are some tips for creating a daily practice:

☐ Schedule it in your calendar: Treat your meditation time like an important meeting. Block the time in your daily plan and stick to it as much as possible.

☐ Find a quiet space: Minimize interruptions by picking a quiet place in your home or office where you won't be bothered. Even a small spot can work!

- [ ] Set a timer: Use a timer to ensure you don't spend the entire process thinking about how much time has passed.

- [ ] Start small and build gradually: As mentioned earlier, begin with just a few minutes a day and gradually increase the length as you become more comfortable. Even short exercises can have a cumulative impact on your well-being.

- [ ] Be flexible: Life can get busy, and there will be days when you miss your meditation time. Don't beat yourself up! Just resume practice the next day. Consistency, not accuracy, is the key.

Overcoming Obstacles and Challenges

Everyone meets hurdles in building a mindfulness practice. Rest assured, this is normal! The following problems are common:

- [ ] Restlessness and Boredom: Our minds are accustomed to constant input, so sitting with our thoughts in silence can originally feel uncomfortable or dull. It's like asking a sugar-craving child to quickly switch to clear water. Be patient with yourself. The initial pain will lessen with practice.

- [ ] Self-Criticism: The voice of your inner reviewer might chime in with thoughts like, "I'm bad at this," or "My mind is too busy." Remember, mindfulness isn't about having a perfectly still mind. It's about noticing the distraction and gently returning your attention to your breath or your chosen meditation center. Self-compassion is key here. Acknowledge the critical thoughts without judgment, and then kindly shift your attention.

- ☐ Lack of Motivation: Life can get busy, and meditation can easily get pushed down the priority list. Scheduling your practice in advance, like you would an important meeting, can help ensure you cut out the time. Setting realistic goals, like starting with just 2 minutes a day, can also feel more doable.

- ☐ Uncertainty: You might question whether you're "doing it right" or if your practice is making a difference. It's helpful to remember that mindfulness is a skill that takes time and commitment to acquire. Just like learning a new language, there will be times of anger and doubt. Trust the process, and pay attention to the small changes in your focus, mental regulation, and general well-being over time.

Strategies for Overcoming Challenges:

- ☐ Start Small: Begin with short lessons, as little as 2-5 minutes, to avoid feeling overloaded. Gradually increase from there.

- ☐ Vary Your Practices: Experiment with different types of exercises until you find ones that connect with you.

- ☐ Use Guided Meditations: Apps and websites provide guided meditations of various lengths, topics, and styles.

- ☐ Practice at Different Times: Find the time of day that works best for your attention and energy levels.

- ☐ Reframe Resistance: View thoughts like, "I don't have time" or "I can't focus" as simply observations of your mind, not facts that must be followed.

- ☐ Cultivate Self-Compassion: Be kind to yourself! Mindfulness isn't about perfection, it's about showing up and meeting your experience with kindness.

- ☐ Join a Group: Consider joining a meditation class or group – community support can be priceless.

Important Reminders:

☐ Progress, not Perfection: Some days will feel easier than others. Focus on the long-term trend, not any lesson.

☐ Mindfulness in the Moments: Even when you miss a regular sit-down meditation, find moments of awareness throughout your day as informal exercise.

☐ There's No Right Way: Trust your knowledge. What works for you is the right way to practice.

Building a business takes both drive and focus. Celebrate your wins, be gentle with yourself on difficult days, and above all, keep showing up. The most powerful changes happen through the consistent effort to return to the present time and time again.

Chapter 12: Beyond Meditation: Living Mindfully

While formal meditation practice provides a crucial foundation, the true power of mindfulness rests in its integration throughout your day. Mindfulness isn't about retreating from the world, but rather, approaching your daily experiences with increased awareness, presence, and intention. This chapter will guide you in translating the skills you've cultivated on your meditation cushion into the diverse moments of your ordinary life.

Bringing Mindfulness to Daily Activities

Life is made up of seemingly banal duties and interactions – brushing our teeth, washing the dishes, commuting to work, and engaging in conversations. With mindfulness, these ordinary acts become opportunities for cultivating deeper awareness and appreciation. Here's how to imbue them with mindfulness:

- Single-Tasking: In our multitasking world, focused attention is a precious commodity. Choose one activity at a time and give it your undivided presence. Even with a routine task like showering, note the sensations of the water on your skin, the fragrance of your detergent, and the process of cleansing your body.

- [ ] Engaging Your Senses: Tune into the sensory symphony of your daily experiences. While consuming, savor the flavors, textures, and aromas of your cuisine. During your commute, consciously observe the sights, noises, and scents around you rather than getting lost in thought.

- [ ] contemplative Transitions: Build contemplative pauses into transitions between activities. Take a few steady breaths before stepping into a meeting, walking out the door, or commencing a new task. This creates a sense of spaciousness and prevents racing on automatic.

- [ ] The Power of Pauses: Schedule brief mindfulness pauses throughout your day. Step away from your workstation, close your eyes, and bring your attention to the physical sensations in your body, or simply concentrate on your breath for a few minutes.

Benefits of Mindful Activities:

- [ ] Reduced Stress: Cultivating a mindful presence in ordinary moments diminishes automatic reactivity, leading to greater calm.

- Enhanced Enjoyment: Simple activities become a source of unanticipated delight and appreciation when infused with mindfulness.

- Improved Relationships: By being completely present with others, you strengthen connections and reduce miscommunication.

- Living in the Present: Mindfulness anchors you in the present moment, reducing rumination about the past or concern about the future.

Making Mindful Choices

Mindfulness empowers you to bring conscious intention to the myriad choices you make throughout your day. From the moment your alarm clock sounds to the way you decompress before bed, mindfulness can transform decision-making into an act of self-alignment.

- The Morning Routine: Instead of striking default as you wake up, pause for a few moments before checking your phone. Notice your body's sensations, the nature of your thoughts, and your emotional state. Set an intention for how you'd like your day to unfold.

- Mindful Consumption: Whether it's food, technology, or the news, apply mindful awareness to what you consume and how it affects you. Before browsing through social media, ask yourself, "Will this nourish me, or add to my mental clutter?"

☐ Values-Based Choices: Identify your fundamental values – whether it's kindness, creativity, personal development, or something else that defines what matters profoundly to you. Use your values as a compass to guide your choices.

☐ Responding, Not Reacting: When confronted with challenges or stressful situations, halt before habitually reacting. Take a few steady breaths, connect to your body's sensations, and ask yourself, "What response aligns with my values and supports my well-being?"

Benefits of Mindful Choices

☐ Greater Self-Awareness: You gain clarity about your values, priorities, and what genuinely supports your well-being.

☐ Reduced Regret: By aligning your choices with your values, you live with less regret and increased self-trust.

☐ Breaking Harmful Habits: Increased awareness empowers you to step out of automatic patterns and choose actions that support your health and happiness.

☐ Inner serenity: When your actions reflect your values, you experience a greater sense of integrity and inner serenity.

The Journey of Mindful Living

Living mindfully is a continuous practice, not a destination. There will be times when you neglect to be present or make choices that feel out of sync. Don't let this discourage you. Mindfulness practice cultivates self-compassion, allowing you to begin anew in each moment without judgment.

Embrace the journey of incorporating mindfulness into all aspects of your existence. By doing so, you'll discover a more authentic, purposeful, and joy-filled way of being in the world.

Chapter 13: When to Seek Professional Help

Mindfulness is a potent instrument for self-understanding, fostering resilience, and enhancing overall well-being. However, it's crucial to recognize that it's not a substitute for professional mental health treatment for certain conditions. This chapter attempts to clarify the role of mindfulness in managing mental health challenges, when to seek professional support, and how the two can work in tandem to facilitate your voyage toward healing.

Mindfulness as a Complement to Therapy

Mindfulness practices can be an immensely valuable complement to traditional psychotherapy for anxiety, depression, ADD, PTSD, and other mental health diagnoses. Here's how mindfulness can augment your therapeutic process:

- ☐ Enhanced Self-Awareness: Mindfulness cultivates a perceptive observation of your thoughts, emotions, and body sensations. This deepened self-awareness allows you to identify patterns, triggers, and reactions with greater clarity.

These insights can then be shared during therapy sessions, leading to more productive explorations and tailored interventions. Therapists can help you decode the messages your mind and body are sending you, uncovering underlying beliefs and emotional responses that contribute to your challenges.

☐ Improved Emotional Regulation: Mindfulness practices like focused breathing and body scan meditations equip you with techniques to manage difficult emotions healthily. By observing your emotions without judgment and learning to tolerate emotional distress, you can develop greater emotional resilience. Therapists can teach you additional coping mechanisms and help you practice employing them in real-life situations.

☐ Reduced Reactivity: Mindfulness fosters a sense of space between stimulus and response. You learn to observe your thoughts and feelings without immediately getting wrapped up in them or acting impulsively. This enables you to respond more methodically and skillfully to challenging situations. Therapists can help you identify your typical patterns of reactivity and develop strategies for interrupting these automatic responses.

- ☐ Greater Self-Compassion: Mindfulness cultivates compassion and acceptance towards yourself. Through practices like loving-kindness meditation, you learn to view yourself with a more compassionate lens, even amidst faults and imperfections. This can be particularly useful for individuals struggling with self-criticism or humiliation, which are often underlying factors in many mental health challenges. Therapists can provide a secure and supportive space to investigate self-compassion practices and integrate them into your daily life.

- ☐ Embodiment: Particularly for trauma-related conditions, mindfulness can support reconnecting with your body safely and gradually. This helps reconcile the fragmented sense of self and reestablish a grounded sense of safety in the present moment.

- ☐ Relapse Prevention: Consistent mindfulness practice after concluding therapy can substantially reduce the risk of relapse for conditions like depression, anxiety, and addiction. It offers ongoing tools for managing stress, perceiving warning signs, and deploying healthy coping mechanisms.

☐ Therapists Utilizing Mindfulness: Many therapists now incorporate elements of mindfulness into their treatment modalities. Some therapy approaches, like Mindfulness-Based Cognitive Therapy (MBCT) or Acceptance and Commitment Therapy (ACT), explicitly integrate mindfulness principles with established therapeutic techniques.

Knowing Your Limits

While mindfulness offers significant benefits, there are instances where obtaining professional mental health support is vital. Here's an honest evaluation of when it's time to seek additional help:

☐ Severity of Symptoms: If you experience overwhelming emotional distress, such as debilitating anxiety, severe depression, uncontrollable aggression, or frequent panic attacks, it's essential to seek immediate professional assistance. While mindfulness can be a long-term support strategy for managing these conditions, it's not suited to managing acute mental health crises. A mental health professional can provide immediate support, assess the severity of your symptoms, and devise a personalized treatment plan that might include medication, therapy, and mindfulness practices.

☐ Trauma: Complex or significant trauma often requires specialized therapeutic approaches like EMDR (Eye Movement Desensitization and Reprocessing) or Somatic Experiencing. These modalities can help you process and recover from past traumatic experiences in a safe and controlled environment. Mindfulness may be a valuable complement to these modalities, but it's advisable to work with a trauma-informed therapist who is trained in these specific techniques. They can create a secure therapeutic space to investigate your trauma and develop effective coping mechanisms.

☐ Difficulty with Daily Functioning: If your mental health challenges substantially impact your ability to function in daily life, such as maintaining relationships, holding a job, or taking care of basic needs, seeking professional assistance is crucial. A therapist can help you strategize to manage symptoms and improve your overall well-being.

☐ Feeling Lost or Overwhelmed: Navigating mental health challenges can be incredibly difficult. If you feel overwhelmed, alone, or like you're unable to manage on your own, there's no shame in seeking assistance. Therapists provide a secure and supportive space to process your emotions, develop healthy coping mechanisms, and find support on your healing journey. They can also offer guidance on various mindfulness techniques and resources that can complement your therapy.

☐ Diagnosis: If you suspect you may have a mental health diagnosis like anxiety disorder, severe depression, ADD/ADHD, or PTSD, seeking professional evaluation is crucial. A diagnosis provides a framework for comprehending your challenges and accessing the most appropriate treatment options.

☐ Limited Progress: While consistent mindfulness practice offers benefits to most people, if you discover that your symptoms are not improving or are worsening, it's best to consult with a mental health professional. They can assess whether additional support, medication, or alternative interventions are required.

☐ Overwhelmed: Navigating mental health challenges can be immensely challenging. If you feel overwhelmed, alone, or like you're unable to manage, there's no guilt in seeking help. Therapists provide a secure space to process emotions, develop coping mechanisms, and find support on your healing journey.

☐ Medication: Mindfulness cannot replace medication for certain conditions. If medication is recommended as part of your treatment plan, it's essential to consult with a psychiatrist or doctor.

Mindfulness and Therapy: A Partnership

It's crucial to view mindfulness and therapy not as competing strategies, but as complementary practices that can synergistically enhance your overall well-being. Here's how:

Candid Communication: If you practice mindfulness, inform your therapist. Discuss insights acquired from your practice, and how they might integrate mindfulness techniques into your sessions.

Mindfulness-Informed Therapists: Consider pursuing a therapist who understands and incorporates mindfulness principles into their approach. This facilitates a collaborative integration of these powerful instruments.

Resources: Your therapist can offer reliable resources about mindfulness, recommend guided meditations, or suggest appropriate mindfulness groups to support your ongoing practice.

Remember: Seeking assistance is a sign of strength, not frailty. There's no stigma in prioritizing your mental health and accessing the support you need to flourish. Mindfulness can be a crucial component of your journey, alongside the guidance and expertise of a qualified professional.

Conclusion

The Path to Transformation

As you reach the end of this book, it's essential to remember that your mindfulness journey doesn't conclude here – it's just beginning. True transformation isn't merely a destination, but an ongoing process of learning, practicing, and adapting. Mindfulness isn't about eradicating anxiety, depression, ADD, or trauma from your existence. It's about altering how you relate to them. Through mindfulness, you can reduce the hold of these challenges and discover profound resilience, even amidst difficult experiences.

Continuing on Your Journey

Cultivating a consistent mindfulness practice is essential to sustained progress. Here's how to establish and maintain your practice as a lifelong tool:

☐ Set Realistic Expectations: Transformation takes time and dedication. Don't become discouraged by setbacks or "good" vs. "bad" meditation days.

- ☐ brief and Frequent: Integrating brief mindfulness sessions throughout the day can be more sustainable than attempting to sustain long practices initially. Aim for 5-10 minutes several times a day.

- ☐ Community Support: Seek out mindfulness groups, seminars, or online communities where you can connect with others on a similar journey.

- ☐ Adaptability: As you gain experience, you may want to experiment with various meditation techniques or integrate mindfulness into other aspects of your life. Trust your gut and choose practices that resonate with you.

The Transformative Power of Mindfulness

The consistent practice of mindfulness has the potential to reshape your existence in innumerable ways:

- ☐ Self-Understanding: Gaining insight into your thoughts, emotions, and impulses promotes a stronger sense of self and a greater understanding of your mental health challenges.

- ☐ Enhanced Focus: The ability to anchor your attention in the present moment strengthens your ability to concentrate, enhancing work efficiency, study practices, and quality of life.

- Improved Relationships: As self-awareness develops, so does your ability to communicate mindfully and navigate relationships with greater skill and compassion.

- Stress Resilience: Mindfulness reduces reactivity and cultivates a less entangled relationship with challenging thoughts and emotions, increasing your capacity to manage life's inevitable stressors.

- Self-Compassion: Perhaps the most profound gift of mindfulness is the cultivation of self-compassion – a compassionate, understanding stance towards yourself, especially in the face of difficulty.

The journey may not always be simple. At times you might feel discouraged, dubious of your progress, or like your old patterns are relentlessly resurfacing. That's acceptable, and it's part of the process. Remember that mindfulness is a skill to be cultivated. The basic act of noticing when your attention has drifted and delicately guiding it back to your chosen focus is, in itself, a significant accomplishment.

Resources for Further Learning

Your journey of learning and self-discovery doesn't have to end with this book. Here are reputable sources for further inspiration and guidance:

Books: Explore the extensive library of mindfulness resources. Some essential authors to consider:

Jon Kabat-Zinn ("Full Catastrophe Living," "Wherever You Go, There You Are")
Tara Brach ("Radical Acceptance," "True Refuge")
Sharon Salzberg ("Real Happiness," "Lovingkindness")
Apps: Utilize technology to assist your practice. Consider reputable programs like:

- Headspace
- Calm
- Insight Timer
- Waking Up

Mindful.org: Offers articles, resources, and access to teachers
The Greater Good Science Center (Berkeley): Features the latest mindfulness research and practices.
Retreats and Workshops: Immerse yourself in a guided mindfulness experience at a silent retreat or mindfulness-focused workshop.

You possess remarkable potential for interior growth and resilience. Mindfulness, with its emphasis on non-judgmental awareness, self-compassion, and skillful responding, offers you a potent arsenal for navigating life's inevitable ups and downs. As you continue on this path, trust the process, be kind to yourself, and celebrate even the smallest moments of clarity and serenity. Whatever change you desire is within reach.

May you find increasing calm, clarity, and well-being through the transformative practice of mindfulness.